Dear Parent:
Your child's love of reading starts here!

I Can Read Books have introduced children to the joy of reading since 1957. Featuring award-winning authors and illustrators and a fabulous cast of beloved characters, I Can Read Books set the standard for beginning readers. From books your child reads with you to the first books they read alone, there are I Can Read Books for every stage of reading:

SHARED READING
Basic language, word repetition, and whimsical illustrations, ideal for sharing with your emergent reader

BEGINNING READING
Short sentences, familiar words, and simple concepts for children eager to read on their own

READING WITH HELP
Engaging stories, longer sentences, and language play for developing readers

READING ALONE
Complex plots, challenging vocabulary, and high-interest topics for the independent reader

ADVANCED READING
Short paragraphs, chapters, and exciting themes for the perfect bridge to chapter books

Every child learns in a different way and at their own speed. Some read through each level in order. Others go back and forth between levels and read favorite books again and again. You can help your young reader improve and become more confident by encouraging their own interests and abilities.

A lifetime of discovery begins with the magical words, **"I Can Read!"**

An I Can Read Book™

HALLOWEEN HOWLS

Holiday Poetry

selected by Lee Bennett Hopkins
pictures by Stacey Schuett

HarperCollins*Publishers*

ACKNOWLEDGMENTS

Thanks are due to the following for use of works that appear in this collection:

Sandra Gilbert Brüg for "The Best Trick." Used by permission of the author, who controls all rights.

Craig Crist-Evans for "My Pumpkin." Used by permission of the author, who controls all rights.

Curtis Brown, Ltd., for "Costume Hour" and "Going Ghosting" by Rebecca Kai Dotlich; copyright © 2005 by Rebecca Kai Dotlich. "12:01 A.M." by Lee Bennett Hopkins; copyright © 1993 by Lee Bennett Hopkins. "Sweet Tooth" by Candace Pearson; copyright © 2005 by Candace Pearson. "On Halloween" by Jane Yolen; copyright © 2005 by Jane Yolen. All used by permission of Curtis Brown, Ltd.

Maria Fleming for "Night Noises." Used by permission of the author, who controls all rights.

Joan Bransfield Graham for "Night Delight." Used by permission of the author, who controls all rights.

Virginia Kroll for "Something's Coming." Used by permission of the author, who controls all rights.

Michele Krueger for "Trick-or-Treating." Used by permission of the author, who controls all rights.

Natasha Wing for "Black Cat." Used by permission of the author, who controls all rights.

Halloween Howls: Holiday Poetry Text copyright © 2005 by Lee Bennett Hopkins Illustrations copyright © 2005 by Stacey Schuett All rights reserved. No part of this book may be used or reproduced in any manner whatsoever without written permission except in the case of brief quotations embodied in critical articles and reviews. Printed in the United States of America. For information address HarperCollins Children's Books, a division of HarperCollins Publishers, 1350 Avenue of the Americas, New York, NY 10019. www.harperchildrens.com

Library of Congress Cataloging-in-Publication Data

Halloween howls : holiday poetry / selected by Lee Bennett Hopkins ; pictures by Stacey Schuett.— 1st ed.
    p.   cm. — (An I can read book)
   ISBN 0-06-008060-4 — ISBN 0-06-008061-2 (lib. bdg.)
    1. Halloween—Juvenile poetry. 2. Children's poetry, American. I. Hopkins, Lee Bennett. II. Schuett, Stacey. III. Series.
PS595.H35H338 2005
811.008'0334—dc22   2004022513
                                                 CIP
                                                 AC

·1 2 3 4 5 6 7 8 9 10 ❖ First Edition

To
Anne Hoppe—
who
howls
poetry
—L.B.H.

For Riley, who loves monsters
—S.S.

CONTENTS

Something's Coming

BY VIRGINIA KROLL

Smell of smoke

from wood-burning stoves,

ripe red apples,

crushed black cloves,

crunchy leaves of brown and gold,

pumpkins bigger than I can hold,

spookiest masks I've ever seen—

something's coming—

HALLOWEEN!

My Pumpkin

BY CRAIG CRIST-EVANS

I carve his eyes, nose, teeth.

I cut his hat to fit his head.

For light I put a candle in.

Tonight we light him up.

Some will say he's frightening.

Some will say he's just okay, but

I don't care *what* they say.

My pumpkin is my pumpkin.

10

His smile burns for me.

Costume Hour

BY REBECCA KAI DOTLICH

Out of the box

fly tangled wigs.

Shoes. Pink shirts.

Ballerina skirts.

Pull out a rainbow

of plastic beads.

Grandmother's gown.

A paper crown,

12

and suddenly—
a fairytale Queen
is all dressed up
for Halloween.

Night Noises

BY MARIA FLEMING

Halloween howls

Halloween moans

Halloween rattles,

cackles, groans.

Halloween hisses

Halloween shrieks—

Halloween spooks

whenever it speaks.

Night Delight

BY JOAN BRANSFIELD GRAHAM

Out in a night that is

dark and delicious,

smooth as chocolate,

sweet candy kisses,

dressed in our costumes,

we dance with delight

on this play-out-late,

stay-out-late, magical night!

The Best Trick

BY SANDRA GILBERT BRÜG

The best trick
on Halloween night,
besides shouting,

"BOO!"

Is wearing a mask
so neighbors will ask,

"Do we know

YOU?"

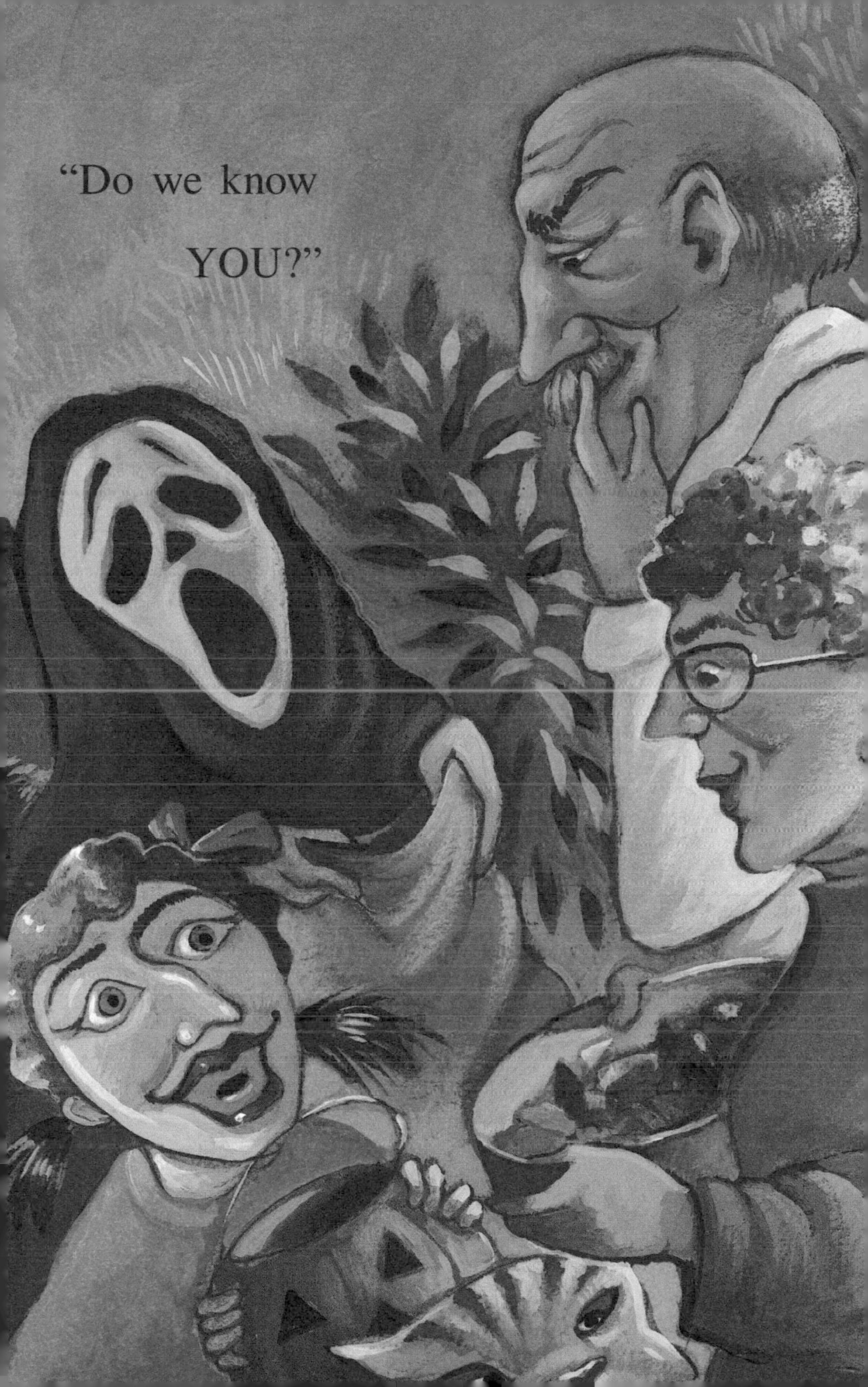

Going Ghosting

BY REBECCA KAI DOTLICH

Gloves and socks
and sheets of white
will dress us up
like ghosts tonight.
We'll BOO, we'll scare,
we'll be a pair
of floating *things*
in stocking feet,
softly moaning, *Trick
or Treat*, till every face
at every door, begs us PLEASE,
"No more, no more!"

Trick-or-Treating

BY MICHELE KRUEGER

Walk and knock,

walk and knock,

all the way

around the block.

Door to door,
street to street,
happy tongue,
tired feet!

Sweet Tooth

BY CANDACE PEARSON

A handful
of loose teeth rattle
in my pocket,
triangles of orange
and yellow
bitten off just so,
nip by nip
to the white tip.

24

Oh, candy corn,

why do you appear

only once a year?

On Halloween

BY JANE YOLEN

One bag of nuts,

Two chocolate bars,

Six sugar cookies cut like stars,

Four candy apples,

A raisin cluster—

Halloween's a tummy buster.

Black Cat

BY NATASHA WING

Black cat

against a yellow moon

casts a blue shadow

on the witch's broom.

12:01 A.M.

BY LEE BENNETT HOPKINS

No more reason

to

shudder,

shake,

shiver,

tremble,

quiver,

quake.

No more reason

for

throat

to

thirst.

Halloween's

over.

It's

November

FIRST.

Index of Authors and Titles